THE COMPLETE

AIR FRYER COOKBOOK

_____FOR BEGINNERS UK 2023_____

2000 Days Simple, Affordable, and Delicious Air Fryer Recipes for

Beginners and Advanced Users

Nancy Any Ross

Table of Contents

RECIPES...**5**

RECIPE 1:   AIR-FRIED RADISH WITH COCONUT OIL 7

RECIPE 2:   AIR FRYER GARLIC SHRIMP 8

RECIPE 3:   AIR FRYER PREPARED CHICKEN WINGS.. 9

RECIPE 4:   ALMOND NUGGETS... 11

RECIPE 5:   ASPARAGUS AND PARMESAN 12

RECIPE 6:   AWESOME FISH TACOS WITH SLAW 14

RECIPE 7:   BANG BANG CHICKEN 16

RECIPE 8:   BASIL EGGS 17

RECIPE 9:   BLACKENED CHICKEN BREAST.. 18

RECIPE 10: BLUEBERRY AND OATS CRISP 19

RECIPE 11: WINGS 20

RECIPE 12: BUTTER WALNUT AND RAISIN COOKIES.. 21

RECIPE 13: CHICKEN 23

RECIPE 14: CATFISH 24

RECIPE 15: CAULIFLOWER HASH BROWNS 25

RECIPE 16: CHEESY BAKED BEANS 26

RECIPE 17: CHERRY TOMATOES TILAPIA SALAD 27

RECIPE 18: CHICKEN CORDON BLEU 28

RECIPE 19: CHICKEN FAJITAS 29

RECIPE 20: CHICKEN PARMESAN MEATBALLS 31

RECIPE 21: COCONUT FLOUR SPINACH CASSEROLE 32

RECIPE 22: CORNFLAKE CRUSTED CHICKEN TENDERS.................................... 34

RECIPE 23: CRAB MUSHROOMS.. 35

RECIPE 24: CRUSTED PORK CHOPS 37

RECIPE 25: EGGPLANT RATATOUILLE 38

RECIPE 26: QUICHE... 39

RECIPE 27: FRIED CHICKEN STRIPS.. 41

RECIPE 28: FRUIT CRUMBLE MUG CAKES 42

RECIPE 29: GREEK CHICKEN KEBABS 44

RECIPE 30: HALIBUT WITH CHILI AND SMOKED PAPRIKA................................ 45

RECIPE 31: LIGHT HERBED MEATBALLS 47

RECIPE 32: MARINATED CHICKEN LEGS.. 49

RECIPE 33: NUTMEG APPLES WITH MAPLE SYRUP 51

RECIPE 34: PARMESAN CHICKEN BREASTS 52

RECIPE 35: PUFFED EGG TARTS 54

RECIPE 36: ROASTED SALMON WITH FENNEL SALAD... 56

RECIPE 37: SNAPPER SCAMPI 58

RECIPE 38: SOUTHERN STYLE CHICKEN 60

RECIPE 39: CHICKEN BREASTS.. 61

RECIPE 40: STEAK AND VEGETABLE KEBABS 63

RECIPE 41: SWEET DRUMSTRICKS.. 64

RECIPE 42: TURKEY BREAST... 65

RECIPE 43: TURKEY CROQUETTES.. 66

RECIPE 44: VEGETABLE FRITTATA 68

RECIPE 45: ZUCCHINI WITH TUNA.. 70

RECIPES

Recipe 1:   Air-Fried Radish with Coconut Oil

Serving Size: 3

Preparation Time: 10 minutes

Cooking Time: 17 minutes

Ingredients:

- 450g fresh radishes

- 30g melted coconut oil

- 2g sea salt

- 2g pepper

Directions:

1. Slice the radishes into thin slices.

2. Place the prepared radish slices in a bowl and toss it with oil.

3. Lay the radishes in the Air Fryer basket.

4. Whisk the pepper and the salt together; then sprinkle it over the radishes.

5. Set the temperature to about 200° C/400° F and timer 10 minutes

6. When the timer beeps; turn off your Air Fryer.

7. Remove the pan from the air fryer. Serve and enjoy your air fried radishes!

Recipe 2: Air Fryer Garlic Shrimp

Serving Size: 3

Preparation Time: 15 minutes

Cooking Time: 25 minutes

Ingredients:

- Lemon wedges
- Minced parsley
- Salt
- Black pepper
- Vegetable oil
- 1g garlic powder
- 453g raw shrimp

Directions:

1. Stir the shrimp with the oil in a dish.
2. Mix the shrimp with garlic powder and pepper to evenly coat them.
3. Place the prepared shrimp in each single layer in the air fryer basket.
4. Depending on the size of the shrimp, air-fried for 10-14 minutes at 400°F, gently shaking and rotating halfway through.
5. Serve immediately with parsley and chili flakes.

Recipe 3:   Air Fryer Prepared Chicken Wings

Serving Size: 4

Preparation Time: 10 minutes

Cooking Time: 35 minutes

Ingredients:

- 900g chicken wings
- Some kosher salt
- Ground black pepper
- Some nonstick cooking spray
- 50g hot sauce
- 60g melted butter
- 4g Worcestershire sauce
- 2g garlic powder
- Some blue cheese dressing

Directions:

1. Make sure to flavor your chicken wings with the right amount of salt as well as pepper. Glaze the air fryer with a good amount of nonstick cooking spray.

2. Set the temperature of the fryer to at least 380°F before cooking the wings for around 12 minutes. Take the fryer tray out and make sure to flip the wings before cooking them for another 12 minutes. Raise the temperature to at least 400°F before cooking the wings for a final 5 extra minutes.

3. Mix hot sauce with butter, some garlic powder as well as Worcestershire sauce inside a big bowl. Cover the wings in this mixture and make sure to serve them warm along with some blue cheese dip.

Recipe 4:   Almond Nuggets

Serving Size: 4

Preparation Time: 10 minutes

Cooking Time: 23 minutes

Ingredients:

- 1 egg white

- 15g freshly squeezed lemon juice

- 2g dried basil

- 2g ground paprika

- 453g low-sodium boneless, skinless chicken breasts, 1 ½-inch cubes

- 64g ground almonds

- 2 slices low-sodium whole-wheat bread, crumbled

Directions:

1. With a fork, whisk together the egg white, lemon juice, basil, chicken and paprika in a small basin until frothy.

2. On a plate, mix the almonds and bread crumbs. Toss the chicken cubes in the almond and bread crumb mixture until coated.

3. Bake the nuggets in the air fryer, in two batches, at 400°F (204°C) for 10 to 13 minutes, or until the chicken reaches an internal temperature of 165°F (74°C) on a meat thermometer. Serve immediately.

Recipe 5:   Asparagus and Parmesan

Serving Size: 2

Preparation Time: 10 minutes

Cooking Time: 6 minutes

Ingredients:

- 4g sesame oil
- 311g asparagus
- 4g chicken stock
- 2g ground white pepper
- 85g Parmesan

Directions:

1. Wash the asparagus and chop them roughly.
2. Sprinkle the chopped asparagus with the chicken stock and ground white pepper.
3. Then sprinkle the vegetables with the sesame oil and shake them.
4. Cook the vegetables in an air fryer for 4 minutes at 400°F.
5. Meanwhile, shred Parmesan cheese.
6. When the time is over, shake the asparagus gently and sprinkle it with the shredded cheese.
7. After this, transfer the cooked asparagus to the serving plates.
8. Serve and taste it!

Recipe 6:   Awesome Fish Tacos with Slaw

Serving Size: 4

Preparation Time: 12 minutes

Cooking Time: 20 minutes

Ingredients:

- 453g chopped cod fillets
- Nonstick cooking spray
- 1g black pepper
- 15g apple cider vinegar
- 15g lime juice
- 8 (6 inch) corn tortillas
- 15g olive oil
- 2g salt
- 50g all-purpose flour
- 15g chopped fresh jalapeno pepper
- 50g yellow cornmeal
- 2g taco seasoning mix
- 800g cabbage slaw mix
- 1g cayenne pepper

Directions:

1. Put the air fryer settings to preheat at 4000F – 2000C, then spray the cooking spray on the air fryer's basket. Take a large bowl and mix together cayenne

pepper, black pepper, salt, vinegar, olive oil, lime juice, jalapeno pepper, and cabbage slaw, then put aside.

2. Take another bowl and mix taco seasoning, cornmeal, and flour.

3. Toss in the fish pieces to coat evenly, then shake to remove excess coatings.

4. Arrange the fish on the air fryer basket at 190 degrees C to bake for 5 minutes.

5. Shake the air fryer basket and bake for another 5 minutes, then place on a plate lined with a paper towel. Put the cabbage slaw into the air fryer's basket to cook for 8 minutes, stir halfway.

6. Fill the tortillas with cabbage topped with the fish, and serve.

Recipe 7: Bang Bang Chicken

Serving Size: 3

Preparation Time: 20 minutes

Cooking Time: 40 minutes

Ingredients

- 67g flour
- 2 green onions, chopped
- 125g omayonnaise
- 453g chicken breast tenderloins
- 64g sweet chili sauce
- 64g panko breadcrumbs
- 30g sriracha sauce

Directions

1. Mix, mayonnaise, sweet chili sauce and sriracha, chili sauce.
2. Coat the chicken with breadcrumbs, Cook for 10 minutes at 204 C in air fryer.
3. Serve and enjoy

Recipe 8: Basil Eggs

Serving Size: 5

Preparation Time: 15 minutes

Cooking Time: 30 minutes

Ingredients:

- 26g basil pesto

- 30g basil, chopped

- 6 eggs, whisked

- 30g butter, melted

- A pinch of salt and black pepper

- 125g mozzarella cheese, grated

Directions:

1. Mix the ingredients except the butter and whisk them well.

2. Preheat your Air Fryer at 360 degrees F, drizzle the butter on the bottom, spread the eggs mix, cook for 20 minutes, and serve for breakfast.

Recipe 9:   Blackened Chicken Breast

Serving Size: 2

Preparation Time: 11 minutes

Cooking Time: 15 minutes

Ingredients:

- 2 chicken breast halves, skinless and boneless
- 4g thyme, ground
- 8g paprika
- 8g olive oil
- 2g onion powder

Directions:

1. Combine the thyme, paprika, onion powder, and salt together in your bowl.
2. Transfer the spice mix to a flat plate.
3. Rub olive oil on the chicken breast. Coat fully.
4. Roll the chicken pieces in the spice mixture. Press down, ensuring that all sides have the spice mix.
5. In the meantime, preheat your air fryer to 360°F.and Cook for the chicken 20 minutes.
6. Transfer the breasts to a serving plate. Serve after 5 minutes.

Recipe 10:   Blueberry and Oats Crisp

Serving Size: 8

Preparation Time: 10 minutes

Cooking Time: 15 minutes

Ingredients:

- 125g rolled oats

- 64g whole wheat flour

- 50g extra-virgin olive oil

- 1g salt

- 4g cinnamon

- 67g honey

- Cooking oil

- 800g blueberries (thawed if frozen)

Directions:

1. Combine the rolled oats, flour, olive oil, salt, cinnamon, and honey in a large bowl.

2. Oil and heat the pan, Spread the blueberries on the bottom of the barrel pan and top with oats.

3. Cook for 15 minutes.

4. Cool before serving.

Recipe II: Wings

Serving Size: 5

Preparation Time: 30 minutes

Cooking Time: 50 minutes

Ingredients

- 4g garlic powder

- 130g buffalo sauce

- 30g vinegar

- 1g cayenne pepper

- 1.1kg chicken wings

- 64g of butter

- 15g of olive oil

Directions

1. Season the chicken and place in a preheated air fryer to cook for 30 minutes

2. Mix all the ingredients in a pan, cook for 5 minutes

3. Place cooked chicken in a bowl, add sauce. Toss well and serve

Recipe 12:   Butter Walnut and Raisin Cookies

Serving Size: 8

Preparation Time: 22 minutes

Cooking Time: 15 minutes

Ingredients:

- 2g pure almond extract
- 2g pure vanilla extract
- 30g rum
- 64g almond flour
- 1 stick butter, room temperature
- 67g cornflour
- 30g Truvia
- 50g raisins
- 67g walnuts, ground

Directions:

1. Beat the butter with Truvia, vanilla, and almond extract until light and fluffy in a mixing dish. Then, throw in both types of flour and ground almonds. Fold in the soaked raisins.

2. Continue mixing until it forms a dough. Refrigerate for approximately 20 minutes after covering. Meanwhile, preheat the air-fryer to 330°Fahrenheit.

Roll the dough into small cookies, place them in an air-fryer cake pan; gently press each cookie with a spoon. Bake cookies for 15-minutes.

Recipe 13:   Chicken

Serving Size: 8

Preparation Time: 30 minutes

Cooking Time: 40 minutes

Ingredients

- 15g seasoned salt

- 400g buttermilk

- 2g black pepper, ground

- 600g chicken thighs, boneless, skinless

- 125g of all-purpose flour

Directions

1. Marinate chicken thighs and buttermilk for 4 hours

2. Mix pepper, flour, and seasoned salt, set aside

3. Dip chicken in flour and coat with bread crumbs after you dip in butter milk.

4. Coat with cooking spray and cook for 25 minutes

Recipe 14: Catfish

Serving Size: 3

Preparation Time: 10 minutes

Cooking Time: 25 minutes

Ingredients:

- 300g Cornmeal
- 12g Cajun seasoning
- 4 catfish fillets

Directions:

1. Put Cajun seasoning and cornmeal in a zip lock bag. Wash and pat dry the catfish fillets then zip lock them.
2. Coat well the fillets with seasoning. Put catfish fillets in the air fryer. And cook within 15 minutes at 390 F, turn fillets halfway through.
3. To get a golden color on the fillets, cook for more 5 minutes. Serve with prepared lemon wedges and spicy tartar sauce.

Recipe 15:   Cauliflower Hash Browns

Serving Size: 4

Preparation Time: 7 minutes

Cooking Time: 15 minutes

Ingredients:

- 453g cauliflower florets, roughly grated

- 3 eggs, whisked

- 45g butter, melted

- Salt and black pepper to the taste

- 15g sweet paprika

Directions:

1. Heat a pan that fits the air fryer with the butter over high heat, add the cauliflower, and brown for 5 minutes. Add pepper, salt, whisked eggs, and the paprika toss in the fryer and cook at 400 degrees F for 15 minutes.

2. Divide between plates and serve.

Recipe 16:   Cheesy Baked Beans

Serving Size: 2

Preparation Time: 10 minutes

Cooking Time: 16 minutes

Ingredients:

- 4 large Eggs
- 56g Smoked gouda, chopped
- Everything bagel seasoning
- Kosher salt and pepper to taste

Directions:

1. Mix the yolks with Everything Bagel seasoning, salt and pepper until well combined.

2. Fold in the chopped Smoked Gouda gently and put the mixture into egg muffin tins put in the air fryer and bake for 20 minutes at 400 degrees.

3. When they are done, carefully remove egg muffin cups with a fork and place them on a plate.

4. Top with a pinch of Everything Bagel seasoning and some pepper before serving.

Recipe 17: Cherry Tomatoes Tilapia Salad

Serving Size: 3

Preparation Time: 15 minutes

Cooking Time: 26 minutes

Ingredients:

- 200g mixed greens
- 125g cherry tomatoes
- 67g diced red onion
- 1 Medium avocado
- 3 Tortilla Crusted Tilapia fillet

Directions:

1. Spray the tilapia fillet with a little bit of cooking spray. Cook in the Air Fryer basket for 20 minutes and the temperature to about 390° F.

2. When the timer beeps; turn off your Air Fryer and transfer the fillet to a bowl.

3. Add about half of the fillets in a large bowl; then toss it with the tomatoes, the greens and the red onion. Add the lime dressing and mix again.

4. When the timer beeps; turn off your Air Fryer and transfer the fish to the veggie salad. Serve and enjoy your salad!

Recipe 18:   Chicken Cordon Bleu

Serving Size: 4

Preparation Time: 20 minutes

Cooking Time: 2 hours

Ingredients:

- 2 boneless, skinless chicken breasts, butterflied
- 4 deli slices ham
- 4 deli slices Swiss cheese
- 64g flour
- 1 egg
- 125g bread crumbs

Directions:

1. Preheat the water bath to 140°F. Lay slices of ham on top of butterflied chicken breasts, then lay cheese on top of ham.
2. Place prepared chicken breasts inside the bag. Seal tightly and place in water bath. Cook 1 ½ hours.
3. When chicken is done, remove carefully from wrapper and pat dry.
4. Bake in the Air Fry chicken until golden brown on all sides.
5. Remove to paper towel to drain. Cut breasts in halves, then serve.

Recipe 19: Chicken Fajitas

Serving Size: 3

Preparation Time: 16 minutes

Cooking Time: 25 minutes

Ingredients

- 453g chicken tenders, cut into strips
- 8g fajitas seasoning
- 1 red bell pepper, cut into strips
- 8g seasoning
- 1 green bell pepper, cut into strips
- 1 onion, sliced
- 12g olive oil, divided
- Salt and pepper, to taste

Directions

1. In a bowl, add chicken, 4 g of olive oil, and fajita seasoning. Mix well and set aside
2. In a separate bowl, mix bell pepper, salt, pepper, and reserved olive oil. Set aside
3. Cook the seasoned chicken in the Air fryer basket for 15 minutes at 3500F as you turn it.
4. In the Air fryer, add bell pepper and cook for 12 minutes

5. Shake occasionally

6. Add veggies to chicken, mix and serve

Recipe 20:   Chicken Parmesan Meatballs

Serving Size: 6

Preparation Time: 30 minutes

Cooking Time: 2 hours

Ingredients

- 453g ground chicken
- 1 onion, finely chopped
- 2 garlic cloves, minced
- 1 egg, beaten
- 2g black pepper
- 2g salt
- 15g parsley
- 15g oregano
- 64g parmesan, grated

Directions

1. Mix together all ingredients
2. Mix with hands and shape into meatballs
3. Arrange meatballs in a greased Air fryer basket and cook for 12 minutes at 3500F
4. Carefully turn meatballs halfway through cooking

Recipe 21:   Coconut Flour Spinach Casserole

Serving Size: 6

Preparation Time: 25 minutes

Cooking Time: 55 minutes

Ingredients:

- 8 eggs
- 150g unsweetened almond milk
- 141g earth bound chopped fresh spinach
- 170g chopped artichoke hearts
- 125g grated parmesan
- 3 minced garlic cloves
- 4g salt
- 2g pepper
- 150g coconut flour
- 15g baking powder

Directions:

1. Preheat your air fryer to a heat temperature of about 375° F.
2. Whisk the eggs with the almond milk, the spinach, the artichoke hearts, 64 g of parmesan cheese. Add the prepared garlic, the salt and the pepper.
3. Add the prepared coconut flour and baking powder and whisk until very well combined.

4. Spread mixture into your air fryer pan and sprinkle the remaining quantity of cheese over it.

5. Bake for 20 minutes. Spread the chopped basil on top. Slice your dish; then serve and enjoy it!

Recipe 22:   Cornflake Crusted Chicken Tenders

Serving Size: 4

Preparation Time: 21 minutes

Cooking Time: 30 minutes

Ingredients

- 453g chicken tenders
- 125g cornflakes, crushed
- 1 pinch of salt
- 28g parmesan cheese, shredded
- 2g Catanzaro cheese, shredded
- 2g granulated garlic
- 15g pesto
- 1 egg, beaten
- 1 pinch of salt

Directions

1. Preheat the Air fryer to 4000F
2. In a shallow bowl, add egg, salt, and pesto. Whisk well and set aside
3. In a second bowl, combine garlic, cornflake crumbs, Catanzaro herbs, salt, and parmesan cheese, set aside
4. Coat the chicken with cornflake mix after you dip in the egg mixture.
5. Cook in the air fryer for 10 minutes, serve and enjoy.

Recipe 23:   Crab Mushrooms

Serving Size: 3

Preparation Time: 20 minutes

Cooking Time: 20 minutes

Ingredients:

- 283g white mushrooms
- 2g salt
- 50g fish stock
- 198g crab meat
- 4g butter
- 1g ground coriander
- 4g dried cilantro
- 4g butter

Directions:

1. Chop the crab meat and sprinkle it with the salt and dried cilantro.
2. Mix the crab meat carefully. Preheat the air fryer to 400 F.
3. Chop the white mushrooms and combine them with the crab meat.
4. After this, add the fish stock, ground coriander, and butter.
5. Transfer the side dish mixture in the air fryer basket tray.
6. Stir it gently with the help of the plastic spatula.
7. Cook the side dish for 5 minutes.

8. When the time is over – let the dish rest for 5 minutes.

9. Then serve it. Enjoy!

Recipe 24: Crusted Pork Chops

Serving Size: 4

Preparation Time: 7 minutes

Cooking Time: 20 minutes

Ingredients:

- 2g salt

- 2g onion powder

- 4 thick pork chops, center-cut boneless

- 1g pepper

- 4g smoked paprika

- 1g chili powder

- 125g pork rind crumbs

- 2 large eggs

- 45g Parmesan cheese, grated

Directions:

1. Rub the pork chops with black pepper and salt.

2. Whisk Parmesan cheese with seasonings and pork rind crumbs in a bowl.

3. Beat eggs in another bowl.

4. First, liberally dip the pork chops in the egg then coat them with cheese crumb mixture.

5. Air fry for 20 minutes then serve.

Recipe 25: Eggplant Ratatouille

Serving Size: 2

Preparation Time: 25 minutes

Cooking Time: 30 minutes

Ingredients:

- 1 eggplant
- 1 sweet yellow pepper
- 3 cherry tomatoes
- 1/3 white onion, chopped
- 2g garlic clove, sliced
- 4g olive oil
- 2g ground black pepper
- 2g Italian seasoning

Directions:

1. Put the cherry tomatoes and chopped eggplants in the air fryer basket. Add olive oil, chopped onion, ground black pepper, sliced garlic clove, and Italian seasoning.

2. Chop the sweet yellow pepper roughly and add it to the air fryer basket. Shake the vegetables gently and cook for 15 minutes. Stir the meal after 8 minutes of cooking. Transfer the cooked ratatouille to the serving plates. Enjoy!

Recipe 26:   Quiche

Serving Size: 2

Preparation Time: 15 minutes

Cooking Time: 40 minutes

Ingredients:

- 125g spinach
- 4g salt
- 50g heavy cream
- 64g almond flour
- 4g ground black pepper
- 283g fennel, chopped
- 15g butter
- 5 eggs
- 4g olive oil

Directions:

1. Chop the prepared spinach and combine it with the chopped fennel in the big bowl.
2. Beat the egg in the separate bowl and whisk them.
3. Combine the whisked eggs with the almond flour, butter, salt, heavy cream, and ground black pepper. Whisk it.
4. Preheat the air fryer to 360 F and spray with oil.

5. Then add the spinach-fennel mixture and pour the whisked egg mixture.

6. Cook the quiche for 18 minutes. When the time is over – let the quiche chill little. Enjoy!

Recipe 27:   Fried Chicken Strips

Serving Size: 4

Preparation Time: 45 minutes

Cooking Time: 1 hour

Ingredients

- 600g chicken tenderloins
- 125g all-purpose flour
- 15g parsley flakes
- 15g paprika
- 4g seasoned salt
- 2g black pepper, ground
- 1 egg, beaten
- Cooking spray

Directions

1. Preheat your Air fryer to 400F
2. In a shallow bowl, whisk paprika, seasoned salt, pepper, salt, parsley, and flour
3. In a second bowl, add the egg, whisk well and set aside
4. Dip chicken in flour mixture, dip in the egg, and coat with flour mixture
5. Cook the chicken in the air fryer for 20 minutes, turning half way through cooking

Recipe 28:   Fruit Crumble Mug Cakes

Serving Size: 4

Preparation Time: 10 minutes

Cooking Time: 20 minutes

Ingredients:

- 1 small peach, cored, diced
- 4 plums, pitted, diced
- 30g oats
- 1 small apple, cored, diced
- 113g almond flour
- 1 small pear, diced
- 30g swerve caster sugar
- 18g coconut sugar
- 15g honey
- 56g unsalted butter
- 50g blueberries, diced

Directions:

1. Switch on the air fryer, insert fryer basket, grease it with olive oil, then shut with its lid, set the fryer at 320 degrees F, and preheat for 5 minutes.

2. Meanwhile, take four heatproof mugs or ramekins, evenly fill them with fruits, and then cover with coconut sugar and honey.

3. Place flour in a bowl, add butter and caster sugar, rub with fingers until the mixture resembles crumbs, stir in oats, and evenly spoon this mixture into prepared fruit mugs.

4. Open the fryer, place fruit mugs in it, close with its lid, cook for 10 minutes, then increase air fryer temperature to 390 degrees F and continue cooking for 5 minutes until the top have nicely browned and crunchy.

5. When the air fryer beeps, open its lid, carefully take out the mugs and serve straight away.

Recipe 29:   Greek Chicken Kebabs

Serving Size: 2

Preparation Time: 10 minutes

Cooking Time: 16 minutes

Ingredients:

- 1 chicken breast
- 3 garlic cloves
- 15g oregano, dried
- 4g coconut oil
- Salt and ground black pepper to taste
- Pinch thyme
- 1 small lemon juice and rind
- 4g greek yoghurt

Directions:

1. Ensure that your chicken has been chopped into pieces of medium sizes.
2. Mix the chicken with the garlic and lemon then immerse in the Greek yogurt and coconut oil.
3. Preheat the air fryer to a heat of 350 degrees Fahrenheit and cook for about 9 minutes.
4. At about 4 ½ minutes, turn the chicken with thongs to ensure the presence of a crispy grill-like coating on both sides.
5. Serve alongside fresh oregano.

Recipe 30:   Halibut with Chili and Smoked Paprika

Serving Size: 2-3

Preparation Time: 15 minutes

Cooking Time: 23 minutes

Ingredients:

- 800g packed spinach

- 2 Halibut steaks of 11oz each

- The Juice of half a lemon

- 1 Pinch of salt

- 1 Pinch of pepper

- 1 Pinch of smoked paprika

- 1 sliced lemon

- Sliced green onions

- 1 Deseeded and thinly sliced red chili

- 125g halved cherry tomatoes

- 30g avocado oil

Directions:

1. Preheat your Air Fryer to a heat temperature of 200° C/ 400°F.

2. Lay two squares of the same size of foil over a flat surface. Divide the spinach between the squares.

3. Season with smoke paprika. Top with lemon slices.

4. Top each fillet with the sliced green onions, the chili and the cherry tomatoes.

5. Pour 15 g of avocado oil over each fish portion.

6. Lock the lid of your air fryer and set the timer to 13 minutes and the temperature to 400° F. When the timer beeps; turn off your air fryer.

7. Serve and enjoy your dinner!

Recipe 31:   Light Herbed Meatballs

Serving Size: 6

Preparation Time: 10 minutes

Cooking Time: 17 minutes

Ingredients:

- 1 medium onion, minced
- 2 garlic cloves, minced
- 4g olive oil
- 1 slice low-sodium whole-wheat bread, crumbled
- 45g of 1 percent milk
- 4g dried marjoram
- 4g dried basil
- 453g of 96 percent lean ground beef

Directions:

1. Mix the garlic, onion, and olive oil. Air-fry for until the vegetables are crisp-tender.
2. Transfer the veggies to a medium-sized mixing basin and stir in the bread crumbs, milk, marjoram, and basil until well combined. Mix well.
3. Add the ground beef. With your hands, work the mixture gently but thoroughly until combined. Form the meat mixture into about 24 (1-inch) meatballs.

4. Bake the meatballs, in batches, in the air fryer basket for 12 to 17 minutes, or until they reach 160°F on a meat thermometer. Serve immediately.

Recipe 32:   Marinated Chicken Legs

Serving Size: 4

Preparation Time: 15 minutes

Cooking Time: 20 minutes

Ingredients:

- Ground black pepper
- 4 chicken legs
- 60g low-fat plain yogurt
- 45g fresh lemon juice
- 4g ground coriander
- 12g ginger paste
- 12g garlic paste
- 1.2kg fresh baby kale
- Salt
- 4g ground cumin
- 4g ground turmeric
- 8g red chili powder

Directions:

1. In a bowl, chicken legs, lemon juice, ginger paste, garlic paste, and salt and mix well.
2. Set aside for about 15 minutes.

3. Meanwhile, in another bowl, mix together the yogurt, spices, and food color.

4. Cover the bowl of chicken and refrigerate for at least 10-12 hours.

5. Arrange the chicken legs into the greased air fry basket.

6. Select "Air Fry" of Breville Smart Air Fryer Oven and adjust the temperature to 445 degrees F.

7. Set the timer for approximately about 20 minutes and press "Start/Stop" to begin preheating.

8. Serve hot alongside the kale.

Recipe 33:   Nutmeg Apples with Maple Syrup

Serving Size: 4

Preparation Time: 10 minutes

Cooking Time: 10 minutes

Ingredients:

- 15g maple syrup
- 30g cinnamon powder
- 60g light butter
- 64g fresh water
- 5 fresh apples
- 50g white flour
- 8g nutmeg powder
- 150g oats
- 50g brown sugar

Directions:

1. Pour in maple syrup, nutmeg, cinnamon, and water in the warm apples..
2. In a bowl, blend butter with flour, sugar, salt, and oat. Turn.
3. Sprinkle the mixture over the apples.
4. Cook in the air fryer and cook at 350°F for 10 minutes.

Recipe 34:   Parmesan Chicken Breasts

Serving Size: 2

Preparation Time: 15 minutes

Cooking Time: 22 minutes

Ingredients:

- 340g chicken breasts

- 1 egg, beaten

- 50g whole-wheat breadcrumbs

- 15g fresh basil

- 30g olive oil

- 50g sugar-free pasta sauce

- 50g low-fat Parmesan cheese, grated

- 600g fresh baby arugula

Directions:

1. Mix the breadcrumbs, oil, and basil and mix until a crumbly mixture forms.

2. Dip each chicken breast into the beaten egg and then coat with the breadcrumb mixture.

3. Arrange the chicken breasts into the greased air fry basket.

4. Select "Air Fry" of Breville Smart Air Fryer Oven and adjust the temperature to 350 degrees F.

5. After 15 minutes of cooking, spoon the pasta sauce over chicken breasts, followed by the cheese.

6. When the cooking time is completed, remove the air fry basket from the oven and transfer the chicken breasts onto serving plates.

7. Serve hot alongside the arugula.

Recipe 35:   Puffed Egg Tarts

Serving Size: 4

Preparation Time: 10 minutes

Cooking Time: 20 minutes

Ingredients:

- 1/3 Sheet frozen puff pastry, thawed

- Cooking oil spray

- 64g shredded Cheddar cheese

- 2 eggs

- 1g salt, divided

- 4g minced fresh parsley (optional)

Directions:

1. To finish the installation, place the crisper plate in the basket and then into the unit. To pre-heat the device for 3 minutes, choose bake, set the temperature to 390°F, and set the timer to three minutes. To begin, press the start/stop button.

2. Fold in half the puff pastry sheet once it has been laid out on a piece of parchment paper.

3. Cooking oil should be sprayed onto the crisper plate after the machine has been warmed. Transfer the 2 squares of pastry to the basket, keeping them on the parchment paper.

4. Bake for 20 minutes. After 10 minutes, use a metal spoon to press down the center of each pastry square to make a well. Divide the cheese equally between the baked pastries. Break an egg carefully on top of the cheese, then finish with a pinch of salt on each. Resume cooking for 7 to 10 minutes

5. When the cooking is complete, the eggs will be cooked through. Sprinkle each with parsley (if using) and serve.

Recipe 36:   Roasted Salmon with Fennel Salad

Serving Size: 4

Preparation Time: 15 minutes

Cooking Time: 10 minutes

Ingredients:

- 4 salmon fillets, skinless and center-cut
- 4g lemon juice, fresh
- 8g parsley, chopped
- 4g salt, divided
- 30g olive oil
- 4g chopped thyme
- 800g fennel heads, thinly sliced
- 1 clove of minced garlic
- 30g fresh dill, chopped
- 30g orange juice, fresh
- 130g Greek yogurt, reduced-fat

Directions:

1. Mix half a teaspoon of salt, parsley, and thyme in a bowl. Rub oil over salmon, and sprinkle with thyme mixture.

2. Cook the salmon fillets for 10 minutes at 350°F. In the meantime, mix garlic, fennel, orange juice, yogurt, half teaspoon of salt, dill, lemon juice in a bowl. Serve with fennel salad.

Recipe 37: Snapper Scampi

Serving Size: 5

Preparation Time: 10 minutes

Cooking Time: 15 minutes

Ingredients:

- Freshly ground black pepper
- 15g olive oil
- 2 cloves garlic, minced
- 2g dried basil
- Pinch salt
- 45g lemon juice, divided
- 680g skinless snapper
- 30g butter

Directions:

1. Using olive oil and 15 g of lemon juice, rub it in the fish fillets until they are well covered with the mixture.

2. Add the salt, basil, and pepper, and place in the air fryer basket.

3. Grill until the fish just flakes when tested with a fork. Remove the fish from the basket and put on a serving plate. Cover to keep warm.

4. In a 6-by-6-by-2-inch pan, combine the butter, remaining 30g lemon juice, and garlic. Cook in the air fryer until the garlic is sizzling. Then pour the mixture over the fish and serve it immediately.

Recipe 38:   Southern Style Chicken

Serving Size: 10

Preparation Time: 45 minutes

Cooking Time: 2 hours 10 minutes

Ingredients

- 1.3kg fryer chicken, cut into pieces
- 1 large egg, beaten
- 403g crackers, crushed
- 2g pepper
- 4g paprika
- 4g garlic salt
- 1g sage
- 1g cumin, ground
- 4g parsley, fresh, minced

Directions

1. Preheat your Air fryer to 3750F
2. Add egg in a bowl, whisk and set aside
3. In another bowl, add crackers, sage, cumin, pepper, paprika, salt, and parsley
4. Spray with cooking spray and cook for 10 minutes, carefully flip the chicken and cook until desired doneness, about 10 minutes

Recipe 39:   Chicken Breasts

Serving Size: 3

Preparation Time: 25 minutes

Cooking Time: 35 minutes

Ingredients:

- 1g paprika
- 35g fresh spinach
- 30g low-fat cheddar cheese
- 226g skinless, boneless chicken breasts
- 15g olive oil
- Salt and ground black pepper
- 50g ricotta cheese, shredded

Directions:

1. Oil and heat the pan, stir in the ricotta and cook for about 40-60 seconds.
2. Cut slits into the chicken breasts about ¼-inch apart but not all the way through.
3. Stuff each chicken breast with the prepared spinach mixture.
4. Spread salt and black pepper to the chicken breast and then with cheddar cheese and paprika.
5. Arrange the chicken breasts into the greased air fry basket.
6. Select "Air Fry" of Breville Smart Air Fryer Oven and adjust the temperature to 390 degrees F.

7. Set the timer for 25 minutes and press "Start/Stop" to begin preheating.

8. Serve hot.

Recipe 40: Steak and Vegetable Kebabs

Serving Size: 4

Preparation Time: 15 minutes

Cooking Time: 7 minutes

Ingredients:

- 30g balsamic vinegar

- 8g olive oil

- 2g dried marjoram

- 1/2g freshly ground black pepper

- 380g round steak, cut into 1-inch pieces

- 1 red bell pepper, sliced

- 16 button mushrooms

- 125g cherry tomatoes

Directions:

1. In a medium-sized mixing bowl, combine the balsamic vinegar, olive oil, marjoram, and black pepper until well combined.

2. Alternating items, thread the beef, red bell pepper, mushrooms, and tomatoes onto 8 bamboo or metal skewers that fit in the air fryer.

3. Using an air fryer, cook the beef for 5 to 7 minutes, or until it is browned and has reached at least 145°F on a meat thermo-meter, depending on how thick the beef is. Serve immediately.

Recipe 41:   Sweet Drumstricks

Serving Size: 3

Preparation Time: 20 minutes

Cooking Time: 25 minutes

Ingredients:

- 4g cayenne pepper
- 680g chicken drumsticks
- Salt and ground black pepper
- 8g Erythritol
- 4g red chili powder
- 15g olive oil
- 1 garlic clove
- 1.2kg lettuce, torn
- 15g mustard

Directions:

1. Mix all ingredients except for chicken drumsticks and lettuce.
2. Marinate the chicken after 15 minutes arrange the chicken drumsticks into the greased air fry basket.
3. Select "Air Fry" of Breville Smart Air Fryer Oven and adjust the temperature to 390 degrees F.
4. Cook for 10 minutes.
5. Serve hot alongside the lettuce.

Recipe 42:   Turkey Breast

Serving Size: 5

Preparation Time: 30 minutes

Cooking Time: 45 minutes

Ingredients:

- Salt

- 4g thyme

- Black pepper

- 4g rosemary

- 60g butters

- 900g turkey breast

- 3 cloves garlic

Directions:

1. Mix butter with salt, black pepper, garlic, thyme, and rosemary in a bowl.

2. Put in the air fryer and cook for 40 minutes

3. Slice and serve fresh.

Recipe 43:   Turkey Croquettes

Serving Size: 6

Preparation Time: 20 minutes

Cooking Time: 25 minutes

Ingredients:

- 403g mashed potatoes (with added milk and butter)
- 64g grated Parmesan cheese
- 1g pepper
- 1 shallot, finely chopped
- 4g minced fresh sage
- 2g salt
- 600g finely chopped cooked turkey
- 8g of minced fresh rosemary
- 1 large egg
- 30g water
- 64 g shredded Swiss cheese
- 150g panko bread crumbs
- Butter-flavored cooking spray
- Sour cream, optional

Directions:

1. Mix Swiss cheese, Parmesan cheese, mashed potatoes, sage,shallot, rosemary, salt, and pepper in a large bowl. Add 50g of turkey and mix thoroughly.

2. Mix egg and water in a medium bowl; add egg mixture and bread crumbs. Stir gently until well mixed. Form turkey mixture into 1-inch balls and place them on a 16-inch-by-13-inch piece of plastic wrap. Roll up and put one crumb side up. Place turkey balls in a single layer in an air fryer basket. Cook for approximately about 25 minutes or until browned. Serve hot with sour cream.

Recipe 44:   Vegetable Frittata

Serving Size: 3

Preparation Time: 7 minutes

Cooking Time: 23 minutes

Ingredients:

- 50g milk

- 1 small zucchini, sliced

- ½ bunch asparagus

- 64g mushrooms

- 64g spinach

- 64g red onion, sliced

- 4 large eggs

- 15g olive oil

- 60g Feta cheese, crumbled

- 60g cheddar

- ¼ bunch chives, minced

- Salt and pepper

Directions:

1. Before combining the eggs and milk, whisk them together in a large mixing bowl until well blended before proceeding. Make a mental point to store it somewhere safe. Mix everything together completely after seasoning with salt and pepper to taste.

2. In a separate dish, add the sliced zucchini, asparagus, mushrooms, and red onion. Tear the spinach with your hands and place it on top.

3. Heat a nonstick pan that has been coated with olive oil and add the veggies to it.

4. Sauté for 5-7 minutes over medium heat, stirring often.

5. Prepare the baking pan by lining it with parchment paper.

6. Pour the egg mixture over the veggies once they have been transferred. Cover the contents of the baking dish with feta and top with shredded cheddar cheese, if desired.

7. Preheat the Air Fryer at 320 degrees Fahrenheit, with the timer set for 5 minutes.

8. When the frittata is finished cooking, take it from the Air Fryer and lay it aside for 5 minutes to cool completely. Garnish with chopped chives and serve immediately.

Recipe 45:   Zucchini with Tuna

Serving Size: 4

Preparation Time: 15 minutes

Cooking Time: 10 minutes

Ingredients:

- 4 corn tortillas

- 1 can drained tuna

- 45g softened butter

- 125g shredded zucchini, squeezed

- 75g mayonnaise

- 30g mustard

- 125g Cheddar cheese, shredded

- Salt and black pepper, to taste

Directions:

1. Spread the tortillas with the softened butter.

2. Transfer tortillas to an air fryer and cook for 2-3 minutes until crispy. Remove and set aside.

3. Meanwhile, in the large bowl combine canned tuna, shredded zucchini, mayonnaise, mustard.

4. In a medium bowl, combine the tuna, zucchini mayonnaise, and mustard. Add seasonings to taste (salt and pepper) and blend well.

5. Spread the tuna mixture to grilled tortillas and sprinkle with shredded cheese and place to an air fryer. Cook for 3-4 minutes, until cheese melted.

6. Serve and enjoy.

Printed in Great Britain
by Amazon